Owens, Bill
Our kind of people

Our Kind of People

Our Kind of People

American Groups and Rituals

by Bill Owens

Library of Congress Catalog Card Number: 74-18225
ISBN: 0-87932-084-2 (clothbound)
0-87932-085-0 (paperbound)

Straight Arrow Books
625 Third Street
San Francisco, California 94107

Distributed by Simon and Schuster
Order number: 21977 (clothbound)
21978 (paperbound)

The author would like to thank Jon Goodchild, Linda Gunnarson, Rosemary Nightingale and Alan Rinzler for their help in putting this book together.

Design direction: Tony Lane
Book design: Brent Beck

Printed in the United States of America by Rapoport Printing Corp.

10 9 8 7 6 5 4 3 2 1

For the past six years my daily routine as a newspaper photographer has brought me into contact with every type of civic, social and fraternal organization in the community. These groups hold meetings at the country club, recreation center or in private homes during which they sponsor luncheons with guest speakers, discuss civic projects and conduct routine business meetings. My presence at these meetings had a purpose: I was taking photographs for the newspaper.

When I started working on this book, I would take the required news photo and then continue photographing the group's activities for the next two or three hours. I also spent evenings and weekends attending meetings, gatherings and musters; over three hundred groups were photographed, some of them two or three times before I got the photo I wanted. After fifteen months I stopped taking pictures and began assembling and editing the captions.

I had enjoyed the experience, but I could never sit through all those meetings again.

Bill Owens

January 1975

This book is dedicated to my wife, Janet, who endured, Pat Lane, who helped select the groups to be photographed, and Alan Rinzler, who said, "Let's do it." And for: The Masons, S.A.C. Board of Realtors, Independent Order of Odd Fellows, Jaycees, John Birch Society, Rainbow Girls, Avon Bottle Club, Roy and Nellie Newfarmer family, Benevolent and Protective Order of Elks, Companions of the Forest of America, Native Sons of the Golden West, American Legion, World War I Barracks 876, Toastmasters, Juniors, Epsilon Sigma Alpha, Supreme Emblem Club, Valley Christian Women's Club, De Molay, National Federation of Business and Professional Women's Clubs, Military Order of the Louse and the Cootiettes, Society for the Preservation and Encouragement of Barbershop Quartet Singing in America, San Jose Coin Club, Maid of Dublin, Beta Sigma Phi, Corral Club, Veterans of Foreign Wars, Christian Men's Prayer Breakfast, Las Damas Club, Soroptimists, Eagle Squares, Pleasanton Chamber of Commerce, Lions Club, Senior Californians, Foresters of America, American Association of University Women, Rotary Club, Newcomers, Voice of the Valley Radio Club, Job's Daughters, Parents Without Partners International, American Business Women's Association, Engineers' Wives Club, League of Women Voters, Friends of Mothers and Babies, Jehovah's Witnesses, Road Runners, Non-Smokers Bridge Association, Tykus, Reach Out, Social Dance Club, Future Farmers of America, American Bowling Congress, Pleasanton School of Comedy, Pacific International Trapshooting Association, Amateur Bike League of America, Amateur Athletic Union, El Chepo Supremo Refried Fhutz Art Freeks Association, Cub Scouts, Blue Birds, Indian Guides, and Kiwanis Club.

Our Kind of People

The *Masons* is the oldest fraternal organization
in the world. We believe in God, Brotherhood and Charity.
We stick together and stay middle-of-the-road.
As a Mason you are never down and out. There is always a
brother to help you.

On July 1, 1973, the *Independent Order of Odd Fellows* (I.O.O.F.), Livermore Lodge No. 219, rededicated its building after 100 years. Charles H. McQuire, Grand Master of the Grand Lodge of California, came and performed the ceremony.

"That you will observe and enforce the code of ethics of the realtor; that you will uphold and support the State Department of Real Estate in its enforcement of the license law; that you will in all your acts be governed by the principles of honesty, justice and fair play. Do you subscribe? You may lower your hands."

Rainbow Girls is an organization that helps
young girls become young women. This is achieved through
spiritual communion with God, service to the
community and the teachings of the Rainbow Order.

We belong to the *Avon Bottle Club.* Clubs like ours exist all over America. Actually we are a little crazy for doing it! We all have shelves full of old Avon bottles.

The *Jaycees'* motto is "Leadership training through community involvement." By working on community projects young men learn how to accept responsibility, make decisions, become effective speakers, learn management techniques and become better employers, employees and citizens.

The Forty-Fifth Annual Thanksgiving Dinner
for the descendants of the Roy and Nellie Newfarmer family
was the highlight of our year. When there are seventy
people for dinner you have to be organized. We have carving and
serving committees, games and a family quilt everyone
sews on. A silent auction pays for the three turkeys. More families
should be proud of their heritage.

The *Benevolent and Protective Order of Elks* (B.P.O.E.) is the largest fraternal organization in the world. The elk was chosen in 1868 because it is distinguished, fleet of foot and timorous of wrongdoing. Our four cardinal principles are Charity, Justice, Fidelity and Brotherly Love. An Elk today is an American gentleman.

When you join the *John Birch Society*
you join an anti-Communist group. We believe in "Less
government, more individual responsibility and,
with God's help, a better world." At our monthly chapter
meetings we discuss local educational projects
that will carry out our national goal of stopping Communism.

The *Companions of the Forest of America* teaches devotion to the home, respect for other people's religious beliefs, loyalty to the American flag and obedience to God's commandments. Our motto is "Sociability, Sincerity and Constancy." Many good and lasting friendships are formed through membership in the Companions of the Forest of America.

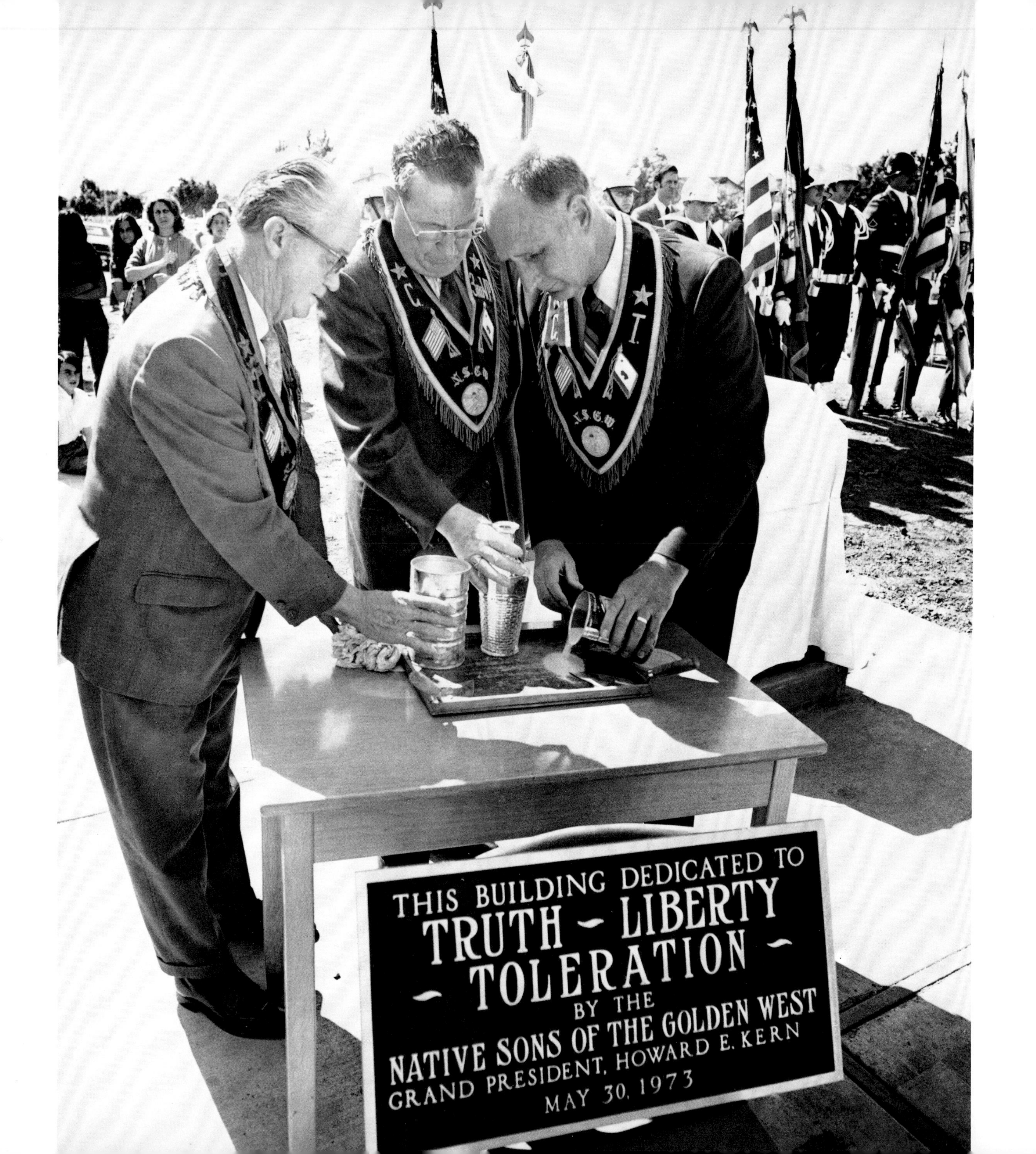
THIS BUILDING DEDICATED TO
TRUTH - LIBERTY
- TOLERATION -
BY THE
NATIVE SONS OF THE GOLDEN WEST
GRAND PRESIDENT, HOWARD E. KERN
MAY 30, 1973

On Memorial Day, *World War I Barracks 876, American Legion Post 47, Veterans of Foreign Wars Post 7265* (the firing squad) and the *Fleet Reserve Association* (Branch 287) performed the ceremony at the Memorial Gardens. Speeches were said with a prayer, flowers were placed by the Girl Scouts and Gold Star mothers were honored. We did all this, but no one cared about the dead lost in the wars. Everyone was on the freeway. . . . It was a three-day weekend.

The *Native Sons of the Golden West* is open to any male citizen born in California. We aim to glorify California's history, support the American form of government and oppose those who want to overthrow it. In today's dedication we use sand from all the counties, water from all the major rivers and cement from Santa Cruz. The mortar symbolizes the strength of California.

694
158
47

The meeting of the *American Legion* and *Auxiliary,* Alameda District 10, starts with the posting of the colors. Retiring officers assume their stations and then leave for the back room. The new officers enter, line up in proper order, assume their new stations and are sworn in. At the county level many blacks participate in the Legion's ceremonies and activities.

ROTARY CLUB
OF
COLORADO
ROTARY CLUB

World War I Barracks 876 has thirty members. Each year the number dwindles as members pass on. We don't participate in community activities; we are a social group. In another twenty years our organization won't exist.

The *Rotary Club* has 752,000 members in 150 countries. It was started in 1905 by a group of businessmen for their mutual benefit. The name derives from the original plan to "rotate" the location of each meeting. Today Rotary is a club devoted to four types of service: Club, Community, Vocational and International. We are still growing and add at least one new club to our worldwide membership every day.

Toastmasters teaches the art of public speaking. At our weekly meetings, speakers are judged on posture, voice, content and emotional impact. The only way to advance in communications is to practice before a group.

Mardi Gras is an annual fund-raising event staged by the Pleasanton *Juniors.* King and queen candidates hold moneymaking events and the candidate who raises the most money wins. Last year we raised $12,800 for the senior citizens' transportation system and $1,000 for youth counseling programs. The climax is the Mardi Gras Ball. Over 500 people come to drink, eat, dance and celebrate the coronation.

Many men like myself step on an airplane
Monday morning and come home Friday night. Weekends
are spent with our families or playing golf and
there is no time for going to church. So the idea of a
Christian Men's Prayer Breakfast group was
great. Our first meeting was held at Howard Johnson's; we
expected twenty-five and fifty-five showed up.

To be president of the Livermore *Juniors* is a great honor. It is also a terrific responsibility. We have only fifty-six members but carry out over seventy service projects each year. I have nine committees for these projects, and the responsibility falls on the president's shoulders.

The Realtor of the Year is chosen by a
committee of seventeen realtors. To receive this honor you
must have made a contribution to the real
estate industry by being a model to other realtors, knowing
the business and contributing ideas and
energies to the Southern Alameda County
Board of Realtors.

The *Valley Christian Women's Club* has three rules we observe at our monthly luncheons: we don't talk about our weight, our age or our churches. Today's luncheon is our annual bridal-gown fashion show. An active membership and belief in Jesus Christ keeps the organization going.

The *Supreme Emblem Club*'s purpose is to assist the Elks in their endeavors and to promote community welfare. The ritual of installation involves three stations: Truth, Charity and Justice.

Honoring your parents, especially your mother, is one of the teachings of *De Molay.* Leadership training, love of country, love of parents and the dress code all help to build character so that young men can become Masons or go on in life with the teachings of brotherhood.

During De Molay Week, members pay respect to mothers who have passed on.

The *Military Order of the Louse* is a veterans group, so-named because many servicemen got lice while riding in boxcars during World War I. The women's auxiliary, the *Cootiettes,* started in 1930. Our first Supreme Crawl was held in Denver, Colorado in 1936. Our main activities are assisting veterans and keeping alive the spirit of fellowship; our allegiance is to the government of the United States of America.

EMERYVILLE
CALIFORNI
LOUSES
BINGO
I AM
AN ALCOHOLIC
BUY ME A
BEER
ALAMEDA
CALIFORNI

The *Society for the Preservation and Encouragement of Barbershop Quartet Singing in America* was started in 1938 in Tulsa, Oklahoma by Owen C. Cash. He wanted to save the barbershop quartet from extinction. Today there are 38,000 members nationwide. Profits from our concerts go to the Institute of Logopedics for children to learn to speak.

I'm known throughout the world as the King
of Coin Collectors. I was the founder and charter member
number one of the *San Jose Coin Club.*
In 1972 the club struck a medal bearing a likeness
of me wearing my famous $10,000 money suit.
I have display and will travel.

At the *Beta Sigma Phi* Halloween party we
dressed like hobos, brought our dinners wrapped in newspaper, drank wine from the bottle and ate out of
tin cans. We really let our hair down.

The *National Federation of Business and Professional Women's Clubs* was founded in 1919. It is a non-profit, non-partisan, non-sectarian, self-governing and membership-supported organization. The B.P.W. is open to all women who are gainfully employed.

OPEN

We drank twelve cases of champagne at the grand opening of the Red Carpet Center. Almost all the businessmen in town came, including other realtors. We ate $508 worth of chicken, ham, salami, potato salad, potato chips, olives, pickles, beans and cheese.

The *Corral Club* is the official greeting club of the Chamber of Commerce. Our job is to welcome new business to town.

The chartering of the Theta Omega chapter of *Epsilon Sigma Alpha* took place at the Emperor Garden Restaurant on September 8, 1973. After the ceremony the new officers were duly sworn in by candle-light. The closing ritual is the Circle of Friendship. The president says, "May we be reminded that graciousness, poise and friendliness are our goals."

The *Maid of Dublin* represents the city at
all official functions—grand openings, ground-breakings
and good-will gatherings. By "good will" I
mean we welcome new business to the community by help-
ing them get publicity.

V F W
POST 9968
DUBLIN

The *Veterans of Foreign Wars* (V.F.W.) gave me the book *Unforgettable Faces*, pictures of all the P.O.W.'s and M.I.A.'s lost in Viet Nam. I worked hard and sold over 2,000 P.O.W. bracelets. I still have another 2,000 bracelets at home.

This is my second marriage and Ken's third.
This time it's for keeps. We were both looking for someone
to be together with all the time. Now we're together
at work and at home.

We had a Russian Orthodox christening of our son, Nicholas Victor Avdienko. After the baptism thirty of our relatives and friends sat down at the table, drank and ate Russian delicacies. Most of our family emigrated to the United States over twenty years ago, and we still observe many of the customs and traditions of old Russia.

The *Las Damas Club* promotes friendship, social conscience and community improvement. Membership is open to women of good standing in the community. We organize bus tours to scenic spots, special groups for gardening and bridge and a monthly luncheon with guest speakers and entertainment.

My wife is a realtor and gets invited to every
grand opening in town. This week it's Sambo's restaurant.

The *Soroptimists* started fifty-four years ago
in Oakland, California. We are now a worldwide service
organization interested in youth achievement
and citizenship. Our yearly luncheon is our biggest fund-
raiser. The money goes to preschool programs,
Senior Citizens and scholarships for high school students.

Druids Circle #111 is the auxiliary of the Druids Grove. The luncheon is our fund-raiser for high school scholarships.

The *Eagle Squares* is one of 100 clubs in the Northern California Square-Dancing Association. We called our group Eagle Squares because we used to dance in the Eagles Hall. Dancing is good, clean fun.

One of the oldest traditions of the *Lions Club* is the "fine," which is collected in a chamber pot called a tail-twister kitty. Members are fined if they goof up by not wearing Lions pins, talking while the president is talking, interfering with the general meeting, advertising their place of business or by being late. We are a civic organization. Our motto is "We Serve." Service is the rent we pay for the space we occupy.

The *Chamber of Commerce* promotes
business and helps develop the community. Our major
activity is to advertise the city and
make it a better place to live.

On Valentine's Day, the *Senior Californians* honored all sweethearts over seventy years of age. We planned the event for months and made it a very special ceremony.

The *Foresters* is a fraternal organization
which was founded in England in the time of Robin Hood.
Each of our new presidents makes his grand
entry differently—one year by boat, once by train and
this year by horse.

The *American Association of University Women* occasionally holds fashion shows to raise scholarships for college-age women. Our organization is active in the community; we have candidate nights, reports on the status of women, observer corps to attend public meetings and consciousness-raising groups for our members.

You have to be at the top of your field
or business to join the *Rotary*. We enjoy the "knife and fork"
fellowship that comes with getting together with other
community and business leaders.

The *Newcomers* is strictly a social group whose purpose is to foster new friendships. We hold classes in gourmet cooking and crafts and get together for bridge, coffee klatches, mah jong and tennis. We hold a fashion show twice a year.

I started the *Voice of the Valley Radio Club* four years ago. We all operate citizen-band radios (we're called CZ's) and have nicknames like Big Mack, Landrover and California Clipper.
A few years ago I saw people wearing these big hats on the Ted Mack Amateur Hour. I just improved on the idea. Now the V.O.V. Top Hatters appear in parades and jamborees.

To belong to *Job's Daughters* you must have a
relative in one of the Masonic Orders—the Masons, Shriners
or the Eastern Star. Job's Daughters brings together
women who believe in God and the teachings of the Bible.
Our group keeps girls off the streets and gives
them social activities and moral training.

Our eighth-grade graduation dance was
really far out. We spent over $160 on crepe paper, stars and
decorations. There was an arched entrance
with flowers, a white picket fence, a fountain with real water
and a black light. We had live music
and a buffet with chicken, turkey, ham, salad, dessert and
punch. We had a ball. You only graduate
from the eighth grade once.

At the *American Business Women's Association* membership tea we staged the "Academy Award Banquet" to honor outstanding working women. We believe in having fun, but our main purpose is to provide scholarships for young women who plan to enter the business world.

Parents Without Partners International is devoted to the welfare and interests of single parents and their children. Tonight P.W.P. is having a pajama party and wine tasting to raise scholarship funds for graduating seniors in single-parent families.

After my first husband was killed in
action in Korea, the *American Legion* awarded me a Gold
Star membership pin. My second husband, Joe, spent
thirty years in the Navy. We lived all over the country and
made many friends through the service.
After Joe died, our two children, now adults, left home to
make their own way in the world. Now I have
to find a job, make new friends and start life over again,
which isn't easy when you're forty-one years old.

People who come to Lamaze classes on prepared childbirth have an interest in themselves and their unborn child. Really, I'm teaching them to touch and to love each other. . . . I've never met a couple I didn't like.

Our *Engineers' Wives Club* called the
annual progressive supper "Dinner at Mount Vernon," to
honor one of our most famous engineers,
George Washington. At four different homes we had Hors
d'Oeuvres Americana, Delaware Punch,
Liberty Salad, Martha's Roast Beef, Potatoes à la Patriote,
Washington Peas, Early American Biscuits and
cherry delicacies. Our husbands did the carving.

A lot of people say we're chunks of meat, like
cattle, but we're not. We're all individuals with dreams and
aspirations like everybody else. Being a beauty
contestant has taught me about myself, other people, poise
and public speaking. If I had it to do over again, I would.

To encourage citizen participation in government, the *League of Women Voters* borrowed a VW camper, put notices in the local newspapers and drove around registering voters.

I worked at the Bank of America for several
years before the baby came. After I left, a number of girls
at the bank gave me a surprise baby shower. I
loved it and the gifts were appreciated.

We of St. Isadore's School of Religion
wanted to make Christmas meaningful to our children. We
avoided commercialization of December 25th
by celebrating the ancient Feast of the Epiphany on
January 6th. Over a thousand people came
to our celebration.

I founded *Friends of Mothers and Babies* after the state legalized abortion. My group is now nation-wide and has its own newsletter. We picket organizations that support abortion such as Planned Parenthood, the American Medical Association, the American Bar Association Convention and many hospitals. Abortion is murder and we want it stopped.

Our informal Bible study group met for
three months. We studied the Book of Job. After we
finished the final chapter we disbanded.

Jehovah's Witnesses are two million strong,
with assembly halls in 208 nations of the world. 37,690
people came to our five-day assembly at the
fairgrounds. At the Saturday morning session 7,330 people
witnessed 321 baptisms. Because there
was no other means, we used a portable swimming
pool for the ceremonies.

Beta Sigma Phi was founded in 1931 by Walter
W. Ross and now has over 200,000 members. It serves as
a precious guard against narrowed friendships
by providing social and cultural activities for young women.
You are never a stranger in a new town when
you belong to Beta Sigma Phi.

Outdoor painters are a breed unto themselves.
Painting in the sun with bugs, the wind and elements
against you is a challenge.

Our new membership champagne brunch is
one of the few social activities sponsored by the *Road Runners.* Our group is one of sixteen units
that raise nearly $100,000 a year to support the Mount Diablo
Therapy Center. We got the name Road Runners
because our volunteer services involved running back and
forth to Walnut Creek.

"All in all, painting outdoors was a joyful experience for both artists in this exhibit. The preview was held at the State Savings and Loan Company office."

The *Non-Smokers Bridge Association*
was started by Audrey Huseman after she had lung cancer.
We hold biweekly bridge sessions. You cannot
smoke during the game; each ante is donated to
cancer research.

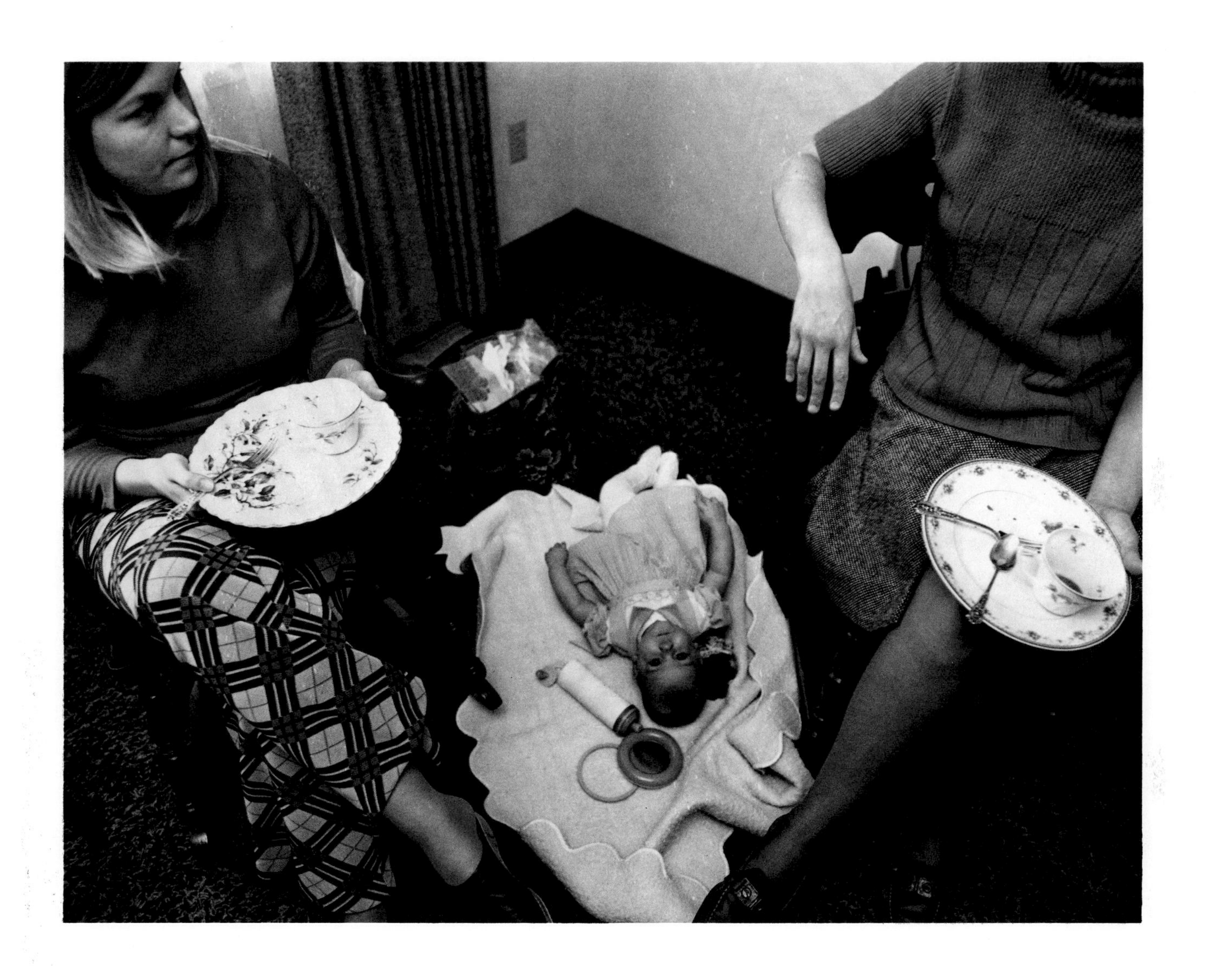

I had the coffee klatch for a new neighbor.
I wanted her to meet all the women on the block. I did it
because I like people.

Our band Tykus practices four days a week.
We're going to L.A. with a demo tape to try and interest
recording studios and producers in our
music. We've put off college for a year and have high
hopes of making it.

Nancy Richardson is a super teacher. Her workshop for preschool nursery teachers, volunteers and aides was an eye-opener. She showed us creative play activities that require simply a good imagination and the desire to teach.

Reach Out is for adults who are single, separated, divorced or thinking about divorce. It is for people who feel lonely but don't want to make the bar scene—people reaching out to be touched emotionally, spiritually, intellectually and physically.

The *Social Dance Club* is for adults who
enjoy "touch dancing." We have sixty members and our
club meets twice a month.

232

A rodeo audience is no longer cowboys and farmers. Now it's suburbanites, city-dwellers and people who like to drink beer and watch the action. They all come to the rodeo in their automobiles.

Future Farmers of America encourages
young people to view the lamb as a commercial object. The
animal is shown so that it will bring the best price.

Representatives from the county and city *American Bowling Congress* were present at the ninth annual bowling tournament at the Granada Bowl. In five weekends 2,500 people competed for $7,000 in prize money.

JR
CHAMPIONS 1971 BASEBALL
CHAMPIONS BASKETBALL
CHAMPIONS 1971 TRACK
CHAMPIONS 1971 SWIMMING
32
35

My prayer is to the god of
football. That's so we will win.

200

I spent two hours driving here, two hours racing with the *Amateur Bike League of America* and two hours driving home. So I really spent twice as much time driving my car as I did riding my bike.

1
2
3
4
5
6
7

The *Amateur Athletic Union* swim meets
are held on weekends year-round. Some 300 families come
to watch and help officiate each meet.

My son Marc is the only serious black junior shooter in the *Pacific International Trapshooting Association*. I think trapshooting is a socially healthy sport, and if Marc becomes the best in his class, it would be good publicity for the P.I.T.A. and for black people in general.

Eight years ago there was one soccer team in town.
Today there are over a hundred with more than 2,000 kids
playing each weekend. We'll soon overtake
Little League as a national sport.

We spent weeks sewing our burlesque costumes
for the homecoming football rally. We wiggled and jiggled
and the students went wild. We were all
stoned on the event.

El Chepo Supremo Refried Fhutz Art Freeks Association—that's the Art Club—organized a wild art show. We got the wedding gowns from St. Vincent DePaul and the boys brought the suits from home. We had a ball.

Basically I'm opposed to organizations like
the Campfire Girls or the Boy Scouts because they put kids
in uniforms and regiment them. However, I've
learned I can function within the framework of the *Blue
Birds.* When the girls are studying birds, I do
a fantasy trip with them and imagine what it feels like to be
a bird rather than take them to a museum to
see the stuffed variety.

When your son is a Cub Scout and is given
a block of wood and told to make a racing car, you know
good old Dad does the work. And, of course,
when derby day arrives, Dad races the car. But your son
gets the trophy and keeps the car on a shelf
in his bedroom.

Under the guidance of the Boy Scouts, the first all-girl post, the *S.S. Endeavor #601* of the Mount Diablo Council, was formed. The girls were active in parades as an honor guard, gave flowers to hospitals, worked on community projects, attended bridge of honor courts and were rated highly. This was pretty good considering they didn't have a ship of their own.

Indian Guides is a father-and-son activities
program sponsored by the Y.M.C.A. It gives you a chance
to be with your son and have fun—learning
crafts, flying kites, fishing and camping—away from the
family situation.

I think *Cub Scouts* need activities. They love tours. Most enjoyable of all was our trip to KYTE radio station where the boys were fascinated by all the equipment and how it worked.

FM
CUB SCOUTS B.S.A.
CUB SCOUT
CUB SCOUT

Lisa has been dancing since she was three
years old. Last year she won fourth place in the California
State Talent Competition. Lisa wants a career
in dance, but sometimes talks about becoming a doctor.

The *Pleasanton School of Comedy* staged a
summer review, "Broadway's Best." Practicing our dance
routines, making our costumes and learning
our songs was a lot of work and it's too bad the community
didn't support our effort. Attendance was
poor but I guess people have other things to do. We still
had a great time putting on the performance.

The *Jaycees* helped me move into my new
home in three hours. When I needed help pouring concrete,
they came again and gave me a hand. I've helped
the Jaycees and they've helped me.

I came home for lunch and caught my girlfriend in bed with another guy. I got in my car and went
round a corner at seventy-five miles per hour. I took
out fifty feet of fence and two trees. I broke both arms,
both legs, fractured my back and smashed
my face. Everyone came to see what had happened.
My girlfriend visited me at the hospital with her
new boyfriend. My car wreck cost $21,000
and changed my life.

000 GENERAL
100 PHILOSOPHY
200 RELIGION

At the dedication of Foothill High School, the Principal, Vice Principal, Superintendent of Schools and President of the School Board each prepared a speech. The ceremony took one hour and fifteen minutes.

KIWANIS CLUB
KIWANIS

The county wanted to widen the road in front of my home. They planned to cut down several oak trees, build a bigger bridge and "improve" the area so more cars could get through. To stop them we organized a neighborhood association and hired a lawyer. Community action works if you hire a lawyer.

The *Kiwanis* is a service organization. We work with young people, assist in drug education, support our churches and promote sound international relations and an interest in community affairs. Our motto is "We Build."

MEMORIAL
DO WE DARE NOT TO CARE?
KAISER'S PLAN is a NIGHTMARE!
PLEASANTON CITY OF PLANNED GARBAGE

IN THE NAME
OF PROGRESS
PIEASATON
DESTROYED
TREES
Call City Hall !!!

The photographs in this book, as in *Suburbia,*
were taken with a Pentax 6x7 camera with four focal-length
lenses—55mm, 105mm, 200mm and a super-
wide-angle 40mm Nikkor lens that was specially adapted
to fit the Pentax 6x7.

All indoor photographs were shot with bounce
flash whenever possible. I mostly used Speed Graflex bare
tubes—one for direct light and the other as
fill-in. These portable tubes give a soft, natural light effect
and are easy to handle in a crowded situation. I
shot 1200 rolls of Tri-X 220 film (ASA 800) which were
developed in FG-7 for approximately ten minutes.

All prints were made by
Chong Lee of San Francisco, a very fine printer.